Barcelona
Tell us about

Gaudí

H KLICZKOWSKI

Barcelona

Tell us about

Gaudí

Drawings by Fina Rifà
Text by Bernat Cormand

Publisher: Paco Asensio

Editorial coordination: Aurora Cuito

Text: Bernat Cormand

Drawings: Fina Rifà

Translation: William Bain

Proofreading: Dave Hall

Art director: Mireia Casanovas Soley

Graphic Design: Emma Termes Parera

Photographs: Pere Planells, except pages 13, 21 and 33, by Miquel Tres; pages 41 and 46, by Joana Furió, and pages 13, 51 and 61, by Roger Casas

Photographs in black and white: Jacint Rifà

Copyright for the international edition
© H Kliczkowski-Onlybook, S.L.
Fundición, 15. Polígono Industrial Santa Ana
28529 Rivas-Vaciamadrid. Madrid
Tel.: +34 916 665 001
Fax: +34 913 012 683
asppan@asppan.com
www.onlybook.com
ISBN: 84-89439-29-X
D. L.: 11.229-02

Editorial project

LOFT Publications
Domènech, 9 2-2
08012 Barcelona. Spain
Tel.: +34 932 183 099
Fax: +34 932 370 060
e-mail: loft@loftpublications.com
www.loftpublications.com

Printed by:
Gráficas Anman. Sabadell, Barcelona.
Spain

May 2002

One sunny Sunday morning, Tim, Olivia, Lina and Toni, the youngest, are sitting on a bench in the square in front of the church that is called the Sagrada Familia, which means Holy Family in Spanish. They look in awe at the church.

"What tall towers!"

"And so complicated!"

"They look like part of a mystery story!"

They want to know things about Antoni Gaudí, the great architect, and to look at his buildings in the city of Barcelona. But they need a guide to take them around. The four children decide to play at imagining what Gaudí was like, and they close their eyes very tightly and think intensely about him.

"He was a rather short man."

"He had white hair and a beard. When he was older, I mean."

"He wore a dark suit and a white shirt......"

"And a tie? Did he wear a tie? I'm sure he did, and a hat, too."

Suddenly, when they open their eyes, there was the architect, just the way they'd imagined. The children start asking him all kinds of questions, but he tells them he's a very busy man and works very long hours building the Church of the Sagrada Familia, and that he has a lot to finish... And he can't answer their questions or take them around to see his buildings. Gaudí then whistles over in the direction of the church, and down from a little cypress tree comes a pretty dove. He knows as much as Gaudí does about the architecture, and he offers to act as guide.

And they leave Sagrada Familia Square

and go in the direction of the Casa Vicens

casa vicens

"Manuel Vicens, a tile dealer, commissioned this house in Barcelona's Gracia neighborhood. He wanted it as a summer house. Look at all the tiles on its wall."

"It looks like a chess board!"

"For this house, Gaudí used the peninsula's architectural tradition and thousand-year-old Arabic art. Do you want to look inside?"

"Yes!"

13

In the dining room of the house, the dove feels right at home.

"The spaces between the ceiling beams are ornamented with cherry branches."

And after picking at a few, the dove adds, "And painted ivy leaves cover the walls and many birds are flying around the door frames. I'm going to say hello to my friends!"

15

While the dove is talking to the birds, the four children discover something.

"A dome!"

"Although it looks like one, it isn't really a dome," the dove says. "Thanks to the paint job, it looks real, though. And anyway, at first sight it looks like we're under a some palm trees."

"How beautiful!"

"Not like this!"

18

And they leave the Casa Vicens,

and start toward the Park Güell

park Güell

"Eusebi Güell, a great admirer of Antoni Gaudí, had planned a model housing development, a city garden like those he had seen on his trips abroad, above all in Britain. The project failed, only two plots of land were sold, one of which Gaudí himself bought. And so the Güell family gave Park Güell to the City Hall for use as a public park."

"That's great! Now we can come and play whenever we want!"

The dove landed on top of the dragon's head at the
foot of the staircase.
"This dragon, with the colored scales made of cera-
mic tile fragments, welcomes visitors to the park.
It's nice, isn't it? Gaudí was very fond of dragons..."
"Will we see more?"
"Yes! And even bigger than this one!"

The children, hurrying along, take the steps in twos until they get to the little plaza.

"This plaza was going to be where the neighbors could get together and also a space where stage plays and folkloric activities would take place. But in fact, we could look at the park as a large theater."

"And the audience?"

"The audience would be sitting on the hillside, where the houses development were going to be built, right opposite the little plaza."

"Here's a bench to sit on. The audience could also see the play from here!"
"Yes... Let's sit down."

"It's got a really funny shape, but it's comfortable."

"And so colorful!"

"For this bench, Gaudí had a mosaic of tiles of many colors and pieces of glass made. And if you look closely, you'll see the form of somebody sitting down. How did he do it? Well, he had a man take off his clothes and sit down in a soft plaster of Paris mass, and that's the way he molded the outline."

"What fun!"

"How would you like to take a walk in the park?"
"That's a good idea!"
The children run along the paths.
"As you can see, the park is like a labyrinth of foot-
paths that go up and down. Gaudí didn't want to
level part of the terrain to make the park, so the paths
take on the form of the landscape. The wall around
the whole park and the bench in the plaza also follow
the contours of the hillside."

And they leave Park Güell, and start for the Casa Batlló

Casa Batlló

"Josep Batlló i Casanovas, a rich textile manufacturer, had a building that must have been very conventional. It was on the Paseo de Gracia. The manufacturer wanted to completely convert the building into a modern one like the houses around it, and he commissioned Antoni Gaudí to dign the changes."

Tim and Olivia and Lina and Toni look at the roof with astonishment.
"It looks like a dragon…"
"Another one!"
"Do you know the legend of Saint George?"
"No…"

"In a faraway country, there lived a dragon that ate anything that passed by, even men, women, and children. To stop the dragon from doing so much damage, the village decided to give it four sheep every day. And when the sheep ran out, they gave the dragon other animals. But one day all the animals in the village were gone, and the town decided to draw lots, each day, another person would be chosen. One day the lot fell to the king's only daughter, and he didn't want to give her up to the dragon. But the village made him do it. When the dragon opened its mouth to eat the princess, Saint George appeared, mounted on a white horse and carrying his shield and his sword, and he killed the dragon and carried the princess away."

"Wow! What a story!"

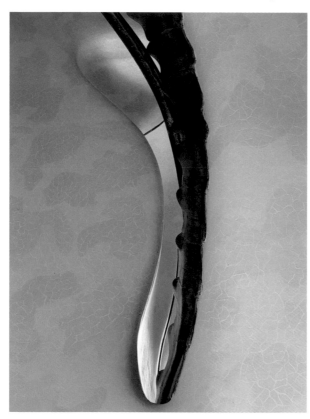

"I told you that story because Gaudí wanted the Casa Batlló to be a symbolic hymn to the legend of Saint George, the patron saint of Catalonia. The roof would be the dragon's crest, a theme that would be repeated in the handrail of the stairway. The balconies could be people's skulls, the ones devoured by the dragon. And the tower crowned with a cross would be the sword Saint George used to kill the dragon to save the princess."

"Look at all those colors!"

"All through the house Gaudí plays with the colored tiles. The air shaft is very bright thanks to the effect created by the tiles covering it. The upper part is a dark blue and as you go down the get lighter and lighter: sky blue, gray, and white on the ground floor."

They leave the casa Batlló and go on to the casa Milà

Casa Milà, la Pedrera

"Josep Batlló, the owner of the Casa Batlló,
convinced his friend and associate Pere Milà to
give the Casa Milà project to Antoni Gaudí.
And that's just what he did."
The children look at the front with eyes as big
as saucers.

"It's shaped like a beach!"
"It reminds me of a really curvy wall!"
"Or a rocky hill!"

"No, it's like a giant!"

"When the Casa Milà was built, the Paseo de Gracia was a place where the wealthy people of the time got together. When they took their Sunday afternoon walk, people stopped to look at it and they showed all sorts of reactions, just like you just did. The house was laughed at in different parodies and satires, and the astonished town gave this building the nickname of 'the stone quarry'."

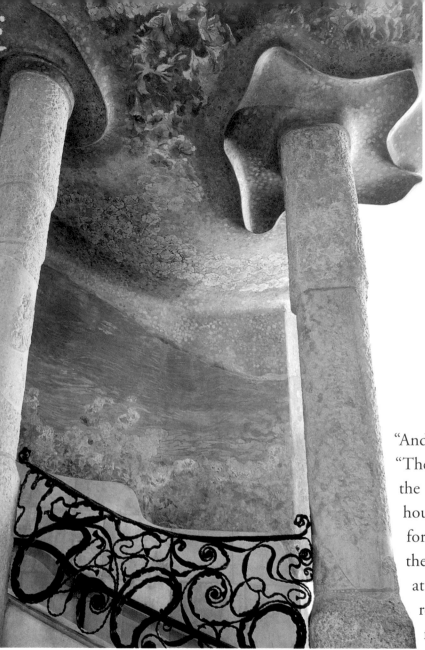

"And what's it like inside!"

"The wavy, unequal shapes on the front repeated inside the house. Gaudí made sketches for each of the rooms on all the floors of the house. Look at the ceilings, the way they're like dunes or like the rough surface of a lake. Going into a house built by Gaudí is like finding yourself in a folk tale."

"Can we go up to the roof?"
"I'll meet you up there!"
The dove disappears through one of the windows, and Tim, Olivia, Lina and Toni stand for a while looking at the windows.
"They look like turtle shells…"

"A labyrinth of short spires, that are really ventilation ducts and chimneys in the form of waves, is at the top of the building. Gaudí considered the roof a space where he could give his fantasies free rein."

"They're like giants..."

"And look at the views. From the roof of the Casa Milà you get some marvelous views of the whole city of Barcelona. Did you know that from here you can see three of the most important monuments Gaudí built? See if you can spot them."

"There's the Sagrada Familia"

"I see the Park Güell! There, on the hillside!"

"And I can see the Casa Batlló, on the Paseo de Gracia!"

"Look! There's the sea!

48

And they leave the Casa Milà and go off
in the direction of the Palau Güell

palau Güell

"The Güell family, one of the most important in Catalonia, commissioned Gaudí to build this as a town house. They also wanted it to be a museum to show their antiques and a perfect place for social happenings and cultural events."

On Nou de la Rambla Street, the four children look at the front of the palace.

"It's so big!"

"Why do you think they had this palace built so tall on a street as narrow as this one? They had it built here because the Güells had a house on the Ramblas and two more where the palace now stands."

51

"It doesn't look like a Gaudí house..."

"To tell you the truth, at first sight it doesn't. If we compare it with other works by Gaudí, it seems a very serious building, above all the façade. Did you see the entrance doors? They're made of interlaced bars of iron."

"And they're enormous!"

"That's right... They made them big to let the carriages pass through. Down in the basement there were stables. Shall we go inside the palace?"

"Yes, let's go in!"

"So many columns..."

"There are over a hundred columns in very different shapes and sizes, from the short stout ones to the slim columns of marble."

Inside the salon, Tim, Olivia, Lina and Toni look at the dome.

"It isn't like the Casa Vicens dome. This one's for real."

"Ooooh! It's like a starry sky!"

"Let's get some air, kids. I'm going to the roof."

"So are we!"

On the roof, the children run through the
labyrinth of colored spires.
"Do you know what these spires covered in
colored tiles are for?"

"They're chimneys!"
"And ventilation ducts."
"They're like the ones on the Pedrera, but smaller!"

And they leave the Palau Güell and go on to the monument to Doctor Robert

Monument to Doctor Robert

"The architect Domènech i Montaner had the idea of creating a monument to Bartolomé Robert, a medical doctor who was an outstanding scientist and also the mayor of Barcelona and a congressional representative. No one knew why, but in the end Domènech i Montaner gave up the project. But the sculptor Josep Llimona was commissioned to do the sculptural part of the monument and he gave the architectural part to his friend Antoni Gaudí."

"The lower part reminds me of the Casa Milà!"

"Yes! It's like a cave!"

"This is exactly the part that Gaudí created. The upper part, the statue of the doctor and the other people around him, is the part done by Josep Llimona. Are you thirsty? Are you hungry?"

"Ye-e-es!"

"Well, there you go, then. This monument has seven fountains and some benches to sit down on."

And they leave the monument to Doctor Robert
and go back to the Sagrada Familia

61

Sagrada Familia

"Josep M. Bocabella had the idea of building a church in honor of the Holy Family. He bought some land for it and, with the architect Francesc de Paula del Villar, began to build. But the architect and the owner didn't agree, and Francesc de Paula del Villar was replaced by Antoni Gaudí. More than a century ago, Gaudí was commissioned to direct the work on the Sagrada Familia."

"But if it was that long ago, how come there are still cranes and builders all over the place?"

"When Gaudí died, the building was at a stage where one of the four bell towers on the Nativity façade had been finished. This was the only one the architect lived to finish. The other three bell towers were constructed after his death, and the rest of the building is still in the planning stage and worked out in the form of a plaster model. The temple is an unfinished work."

"And what will the temple look like when it's finished?"

"It will be a cathedral with twelve towers, like the ones you can see there now. In the middle, the highest one, nearly 560 feet tall, will have four other spires around it. Also, the cathedral was planned as a complex with schools for children and professional workshops for workers all around it. In fact, one school was completely finished."

"But it'll take a long time to do all that!"

"Yes... They say it'll be finished some fifty years from now."

"We'd like to go up one of the spires!"

"We can do that later. But don't you want me to tell you about the Nativity façade, the only one Gaudí finished?"

"OK!"

"In this façade, the architect wanted to express the joy of creation about the birth of Christ. In the Nativity façade alone there are thirty different kinds of plants, and also animals, like the two turtles that hold up these two columns. The turtle on the sea side is a sea turtle, and the other one is a land turtle. There are also stars, and under the eastern star we see Jesus, Mary, and Joseph, with their ox and their ass, on each side and surrounded by singers and angels."

"It's like a gigantic manger scene!"

"Well, now that you've got an idea of what the temple is like, shall we go up into a tower?"
"Oh, yes, please!"

After an interminable number of stairs on a very narrow winding staircase, Tim, Olivia, Lina, and Toni arrive. The dove is already waiting for them. And after they have looked out on the marvelous views of the city, the children begin to feel tired and decide to go back down to the plaza and sit down on the bench.

"Let's see if Antoni Gaudí appears again..."
"You know he's very busy now, but if you need me, you'll find me over there in the cypress tree. So long!"

Life and works of Antoni Gaudí

1852 Antoni Gaudí born in Reus, a town near Tarragona, Spain.

1867 Aged 15, he began to draw for *El Arlequín*, a magazine published in his town.

1873 He went to live in Barcelona, and to study architecture.

1883 Gaudí drew plans for a house for a tile manufacturer. He used many tiles in the work, all very colorful. The house is called Casa Vicens, in memory of the owner.

1883 In Santander, he created a very original house with Oriental forms which people called El Capricho (Caprice).

1884 Gaudí worked for the Güell family. He built the entrance to one of their manor houses and also the stables for the horses. On the door is a wrought-iron dragon.

1886 On a very dark and narrow street, Gaudí constructed a luxurious palace for the Güell family.

1888 The Order of the Discalced Carmelite Nuns asked Gaudí to extend their college.

1889 He traveled to the province of León to build the palace of the Bishop of Astorga.

1892 He traveled to the province of León and drew up the plans for the Botines house.

1895 Near Barcelona, beside the sea, he constructed a wine cellar for the Güell family.

1898 The Calvet Family commissioned Gaudí to build a house near Barcelona's Plaza Cataluña. The house won the prize for the best building in the city.

1900 He drew the plans for a house on Tibidabo. The house is called Bellesguard (pretty view) due to its wonderful panoramic views of Barcelona.

1900 He began work on Güell Park. The house had been planned as an urbanization, but in the end was developed into a park.

1903 Gaudí was commissioned to restore the Cathedral of Palma de Mallorca.

1904 He refurbished the Casa Batlló on the Paseo de Gracia (Barcelona).

1906 He began the Casa Milà, popularly called La Pedrera because of its resemblance to a stone quarry.

1908 Gaudí worked on the church at the Colonia Güell. Colonias were small towns built for a factory's workers.

1910 Well known abroad, Gaudí traveled to Paris to exhibit his works.

1914 The architect dedicated himself exclusively to the construction of the Church of the Holy Family, on which he had been working for 31 years. He spent the last years of his life on that work alone.

1926 Gaudí was hit by a tramcar and died.

Park Güell

CasaVicens

Casa Milà, la Pedrera

Sagrada Familia

Casa Batlló

Monument to
Doctor Robert

Palau Güell

visit the works of Antoni Gaudí

in Barcelona

I look, discover and draw

I like

the doors

the tiles

the chimney

the ceramics

79

Other Titles from the Publisher

Fundición, 15 Polígono Industrial Santa Ana 28529 Rivas-Vaciamadrid Madrid Tel. 34 91 666 50 01 Fax 34 91 301 26 83 asppan@asppan.com www.onlybook.com

Gaudí. Obra completa/
Gaudí. Complete works
ISBN (E): 84-89439-90-7
ISBN (GB): 84-89439-91-5

Gaudí y el Modernismo en Barcelona
ISBN: (E)   84-89439-50-8
ISBN: (GB) 84-89439-51-6

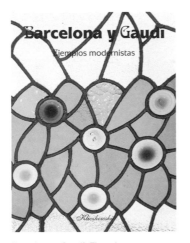

Barcelona y Gaudí. Ejemplos
modernistas/Barcelona and Gaudí.
Examples of Modernist architecture
ISBN: (E)   84-89439-64-8
ISBN: (GB) 84-89439-65-6

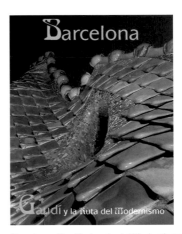

Barcelona, Gaudí y la ruta del Modernismo/
Barcelona, Gaudí and Modernism
ISBN: (E)   84-89439-50-8
ISBN: (GB) 84-89439-51-6
ISBN: (D)   84-89439-58-3
ISBN: (IT)   84-89439-59-1
ISBN: (JP)   84-89439-60-5